AF348614

Reflections

To my husband, my children, and friends that have encouraged me through the years to continue to write and express myself through poetry, I extend my deepest gratitude. For allowing the ink to continue to flow through my creative pen, I give thanks to God. For each person, they know who they are, that has been asked to critique my work I am forever grateful. Their encouragement has cheered me on at each junction, and guided me on the journey to publish this book.

As you read the selected poems in this book, I trust that you will discover the peace and beauty of nature that can be difficult at times to find in a broken world. The simplicity of which nature sings confounds those that attempt to unravel the complexity that breathes from the portals of earth, and brings a certain awe to our world. The wonder of nature gives us reason for hope in a world of chaos and confusion. It transcends everything and opens the gateway to our thoughts for a fresh perspective on life.

Nature Sings

Every component of nature has its own unique sound, a vibration, a song, or some form of communication that allows it to speak to its surroundings. Each voice can be heard whether a whisper or shout.

The robin sings at the break of day, bees hum as they gather their nectar, wind whispers and rustles through the trees and howls in the torrents of rain, water trickles upon the rocks...each presents its own beautiful and yet distinctly different hymn. The placid voice of a flowing stream brings peace while the cardinal's sonnet releases hope at the dawning of a new day. The mating call of some animals will be easy for the naturalist to recognize, but not so much for the book worm. How does the grass know when to turn green after a harsh winter? Is there some oracle that commands the blossoms to open? Does the butterfly hear some soft voice reminding it that it is time to break forth from the cocoon?

All of nature has a sound through which comes the song that brings peace to the troubled soul, clarity to the confused mind, and a hope that all will be well in the span of time. Amid the simple beauty of nature, many find a serenity and tranquility that they find in no other place. I trust that you will watch and listen for the soothing ballads that only nature can play. For the bending ear will hear all of nature as she sings.

Nature Sings

Copyright 2022 by Marlene Tidwell

FIRST EDITION

Cover Design & Layout by Todd Engel

The stillness had settled over the lake as the sky laid the remnants of the day upon the glassy floor. The richest and purest hues fell upon the lake as if some renowned artist thought it to be a canvass. The whole earth stood in a solemn still as dusk sang a soothing song of peace.

Dusk on Sunset Harbor

That sacred passage of the day
When the hands of time will meet,
And upon her silken back is laid
Ribbons of the finest shades,
Across the lake when dusk doth sweep.

It takes me every time
Thru the eye's celestial gate
Where I hear the evening chimes,
Recite the kindest rhythms,
And see the clouds dressed in lace.

Peaceful I shall go
Swaying in the cradle of rest
To see the geese in their rows,
Their little ones all in tow,
When at last the day reveals her best.

My eyes travel to the west
To see the fading sun
Where the day has set,
And the moon will crest,
When the lake and sky are one.

The curtains are now drawn
Over the flowers by the arbor
Where her beauty had been shown
To the evening and I, alone,
Of the beautiful, Sunset Harbor.

The cool evening breeze wafted through the valley and kissed my face. Above the hill, the moon was seated and prepared to take the scepter to rule the night. A silvery mist illuminated the vale between the hills, and every creature of the field. I wanted to walk the country lane once more, but the soft chorus of the trickling waters bade me to sleep; a perfect benediction to the day!

Having being raised in a small town on a farm, these are the summer evenings that I remember. Around dusk the family would gather on the front porch. The old yellow rocking chair was my favorite, but sometimes I would sit with Daddy in the glider. Without hesitation, he could tell me the origin of every sound. With expectation I would patiently wait for my favorite song of the evening to begin to play. Some evenings I would hear it in the distance woods while at other times the white picket fence would be the stage from which the unique song of the whip-poor-will would come.

For some reason, a tinge of sadness clouds my heart when the warm evenings of summer begin to fade into the long, cold winter nights. The voices of a summer's night are vibrant, cheerful and so soothing, but somehow those voices seem to wander into the abyss of silence when winter comes.

Oh, how I miss summer's season when it is her time to hand the specter to the next season. I trust that she will come my way again soon!

Summer's Season

Summer's visit, her last
Night had come to spend,
The year's warmest season
Having always been my friend.
Eve's lamp ablaze in the sky
Sent memories of evenings,
When once I was a child.
Winnowing amid the hills came
Voices welcoming the night,
While the woodland watched the
Whip-poor-will descend from
rosy heights.
In the vale, cradled by the hills,
Summer's blossoms rested
Amid the peaceful still.

What might I do
For this guest of mine
To give a farewell to send
Her into another year of time?
A party I could plan and invite
Friends, or dream in the beauty
Of hope, to delay morning's light.
To Heaven's corridors, a request I sent
To extend the splendor of the night
And for natures hand to relent.
Winter's dress with little flare
Is adorned, only bowed trees
Mourning in their branches bare.

For that passing season, I
Thought my heart would rend,
When I heard the summons for
For the presence of a faithful friend.
Loyal and true I forever will be
In the waning moments as silver
Pearls filter through aging leaves,
And cool waters gently flow
Laying the benediction song
Upon the chords of my soul.
In your presence, will I abide
Until the wings of dawn are spread,
And I bid my favorite season goodbye.

One autumn evening, a most unique scene unfolded over the lake. The sky was clear, vacant of any milky banners or wandering clouds when suddenly there appeared one lonely cloud moving with clarity and celerity, almost as if it were chasing the moon. It was one of the most unusual, but spectacular sights I had ever witnessed. Almost as if this late evening show was just for me.

The two were acting as though they had heard the behest of some conductor in the Heavens as the most unique painting was brushed on the evening sky for all who were awake to see. The cloud had the form of a fisted hand, but once over the moon it begin to break and separate allowing for the rays of light to filter thru the cloud and then fall upon the lake. Each ray was separated by a small sliver of the cloud creating an image that appeared like a hand holding the moon though unable to prevent the light from seeping thru its fingers. It was one of the finer moments of a breath-taking evening on the lake.

As for me, I was so grateful to have been awakened by the cloudy hand!

The Cloudy Hand

Basking in amber glow,
It waned in the evening sky;
The moon at half-mast draped the
Lake, with her regal head held high.

Twas then my senses came alive
Amidst the sweetest dreams,
To see the trailing cloud running along
The horizon to change the scene.

On that starry night
No blemish the sky did show,
Just the lonely cloud to reveal its hand
To silent hills below.

Ever so quickly it heeded
The oracles of the wind,
As if to chase the remnants
Of some long, lost friend.

Beneath the evening's canopy
They exchanged their flatteries
Complimenting each other with their
Colors as they mingled in the shadows.

As though they had rehearsed,
The cloud would break and spread
To sift the light thru its fingers
Like slivers of golden threads,

To glide upon the wavelets
As each would rise and crest,
While the moon and the cloudy hand
Settled in for another night's rest.

It's the time of year when every tree has the pleasure of visiting nature's closet to choose from the most vivid garments. Some choose the stately scarlet coat; others mantle their branches with shimmering oranges while others will decide on the shades of the golden sapphires. The vales proudly wear their diadems of royal purple ironweed with the goldenrod sprinkled throughout the midst creating one of nature's most famed portraits.

With the greatest of care, each tree prepares for this spectacular event with just the right proportions of sun, rain and cool evenings. It is as though the forest has waited all year to display its best for the grand finale of the season. Yet, each one is aware that the chilling winds will come to take their splendor and glory. Then, to spread it like a quilt upon the bed of the forests and fields, in wait for the fury of Ole Man Winter.

Dancing Leaves

In perfect rhythm they danced,
Orange, yellow, gold and red,
Upon their nimble heels they pranced.
The vale in a silent trance,
Watched as the quilt was spread.

Down the yellow lane
They continued to stroll,
Calling out my name
Round my feet they came,
Each one finding a place in the fold.

Most splendid season of the year,
This question I must ask,
Who flatters you with such cheer?
Is it the One that nature holds so dear
That allows you in this beauty to bask?

Please tell me, for I must soon know
Before winter's chilling wind
Drops the clouds of snow,
And autumn's gates are closed
When her pretty face fades beyond the bend.

For I fear I shall not remember
What the Oak or the Chestnut wore,
Nor the shimmering colors of September
Turning into the dismal grays of December.
When all I shall have is a memory of
autumn's yore.

Some entomologists claim that the Monarch butterflies are the most beautiful of all the species. The monarch is considered the "king" of the butterflies, and hence the name "monarch".

They start out as an egg, hatch into larvae (a caterpillar), and then wrap themselves in the warm, fuzzy blanket known as a cocoon. Being nourished for a period of time they are then ready to display their beauty to the world. The monarch is the only insect that can travel up to 2500 miles to migrate to escape the cold temperatures of winter. It also has a poisonous chemical that will protect it from frogs, birds, mice and lizards. Truly, they are one of nature's miracles.

Sitting on the patio on a beautiful autumn afternoon I watched what appeared to be some 30 – 40 butterflies flutter from flower to flower. Perhaps they were having the farewell party before migrating south. Let the poem whisk you away to hear the flutter of the Monarch's wings and see the rainbow of colors that was spread upon that autumn afternoon!

An Afternoon's Parade

There in the arms of afternoon
Enthralled by the beauty and bliss,
Between moments of sun and shade,
When my heart asked to stay
Knowing full well I would without remiss.

Accepting with such pleasure and grace
And tempted to close my eyes,
Suddenly, I saw the monarch's face
Painted in brilliant shades of lace
Seated upon the pedals in summer style.

So pleased the breeze had not lured me into rest;
I watched with eye unflinched as the parade
Displayed the breed's finest and best,
Each wing clasped to create a rainbow crest
As if some timely message they wished to convey.

To think that just days before
Nature's silk had each one concealed
And nourished by winter's store
In preparation to travel to a distant shore,
For this miracle of beauty to now be revealed.

There are over 400 different types of willows with the "weeping willow" being the most popular. Its leaves are sometimes described as long feathers that sway with the slightest of breeze. They lavish water and flourish by creeks, lakes and rivers. The roots are known for their strength and toughness going very deep into the soil. They are also one of the first trees to sprout when spring unveils its green, and one of the latest to release its leaves to the cold, winter's wind. They are a beautiful and unusual tree, and will quickly take root from a sprout.

It is common to see willow trees especially in the southern region of the U.S. The largest and most beautiful willow tree that I have ever seen is firmly established on the banks of a picturesque lake in a small town in Kentucky. When the century's worst ice storm hit in January of 2009, my husband called and informed me that the willow tree was gone. My heart sank and I begin to cry…I loved that willow tree! I could not figure out if he was just excited about getting to use his chain saw, or if the tree was really beyond saving. However, when he sent me a picture, I feared him to be correct. Even with that, I told him to leave it and not to touch it.

On a warm day in early March, a neighbor came and reassured me that the tree could be salvaged…so the intense pruning began! Every single branch of the tree was split, but I held my breath and said a prayer. In one month, the tree had come back to life! I was elated to see the green boughs flowing with April's breeze upon my first trip to the lake. It was more picturesque than ever before especially when compared to the many unsightly stubs left from the ravages of the winter's ice storm. When my eyes met that willow with a cardinal perched on one of its branches, I knew the story must be told and given its rightful passage on the printed page.

The Willow

What verse might I penn
To tell of the beauty of your
Lush green boughs as they bow
And flow in the evening's wind?

On this I must dream a while,
For faithful you have stood when
The billows raged and calmed again
Since I was just a child.

I remember that day so well
When, untimely, that storm came
And one by one your
Branches snapped and fell.

They told me you were done,
And oh how my heart grieved
And prayed for you to breathe
Again beneath the showers
of sun.

A sweet promise you did hold,
A pearl just for me that
Brought such hope that only
My Lord and I did know.

Beneath your arches I stood,
On the eve of Spring, when I looked
To see your fresh green twigs
Just as I knew I would.
Twas then I heard the familiar voice
Of my red-feathered friend for
A new song we would sing as
By the lake we both rejoiced.

Once again you will sway
To the song of the breeze
When clouds gather and
Spread across the bay

To bring me comfort when I weep,
And rock me gently in the
Hammock down
Halls of peaceful sleep.

Spring opens wide its gate for every winter's embittered heart to stroll along its path, and watch the fresh blossoms unfurl. Winter is forced to relent as the warm rays are spread across the earth. The warm breeze heeds the decree to kiss each face amid the beauty of the daffodils. Finally, spring's ballad silences the cold winds and the sweet perfume fills the virgin air. Good riddance winter!

Autumn arrives in early morning, but spring at the close of a winter day.

— Elizabeth Bowen

Once Again You Will Come My Way

The song you sing I do not know,
But it rings so clear thru morning's cold
And reminds me that spring will come again
When the earth will swallow her snow.

Your melody speaks of a distant day
When the sun casts its soothing rays
And flowers open their sleepy eyes
When earth will arise and wake.

Our village is thankful for your notes
Thru the chilling winds you spoke
And gives us cause this wintry morn
To raise our eyes in hope.

But for now by the fireplace I'll stay,
In wait for the warm breeze of May,
When dressed in your scarlet coat
Once again you will come my way.

An Invitation to a Spring Gala

Give her the praise she deserves
Of budding flowers and grazing herds
And let the golden eye arise
To shed beams healing from the sky,
When I shall see the feathers on my sill
And watch the brushing of the daffodils.

A prelude the choir could give
To announce the end of winter's chill
And be accompanied by flutters
On petals as they dance and sputter
Of butterflies with their fancy faces
Against flowers before bowing in vases.

A table we could spread
Adorned with roses of pink and red
And invite the whole town,
And men and women of renown
To celebrate with a fling
The coming of our beloved spring.

So let the celebration begin
With all our festive friends
As we greet them at the door
Returning from another shore
As they sing upon their return
The song for which we yearn!

"The true harvest of my life is intangible –
a little star dust caught, a portion of the rainbow I have clutched..."

— Henry David Thoreau

"The soul would have no rainbow had the eyes no tears."

— John Vance Cheney Quotes

The Painted Arch

The thunder roared its final blast
And each cloud was sealed,
No more rain would pass
As the new scene was being cast
When the sky's true colors would be revealed.

No footprints in the sand to find
Just remnants of an unforgiving storm
That had left its legacy in time,
And to the shore had been quite unkind
And for the loss…reason to mourn.

The island lay in peaceful rest
Amid the sea of gray
When I saw coming from the west
The trestles carrying the waning crest
To offer the farewell to the day.

Across the sky I saw the touch,
As though of some painter renown,
Who held a silken brush,
Stroke colors deep and lush
And twas then the silver lining I found.

There I stood beneath the painted arch
Watching the colors slowly dry
When the song of the evening lark
Left a thankful note upon my heart
To the one who colored the rainbow in the sky.

The Mourning Dove is one of the most common birds on the continent offering a soft, drawn-out call in the form of a lament. It is a graceful, slender-tailed, small-headed bird. Often they come in pairs...male and female. They are known for their fast flight and making a sharp whistling sound with their wings as they take to flight. Their call is soft and soothing, and their eyes are tender and kind.

When I hear their call, I always think back to the spring that my sweet mother made her final quest across the sea of life, I saw doves everywhere...it was as if they were following my every step soothing my grieving heart. When I would travel to the farm in the waning days of my mother's life, there I would be greeted, and at my own home they would come and set on my deck to visit for seemly hours at a time.

On a beautiful day in May, as I prepared to make the journey to that beloved farm and say my final farewell, there they were on my kitchen windowsill. I had never seen one bird let alone two birds of the same kind perched on that small, narrow place, nor have I ever seen any since that time. That place was a difficult and unusual place for any of my feathered friends to sit and visit. But there they were, faithful friends until the end. They serenaded me for the longest time. My husband and son both agreed that surely it was a sign from Heaven to reassure us that my mother was safe and secure in her final resting place!

The Song of the Dove

Your voice rested upon my ear,
From whence it came I was not sure,
But when I turned to see your face,
From the woods you disappeared.

Your refrain akin to that of no other
Offering soothing strains while the
Wooded vales were faithful
To offer you cover.

I heard you in the evening air
When life was fair and grand,
And when the path was overcast
With clouds of somber despair.

My melancholy cares you tried
to smother
When with your trusted friend
You came, on that day when
Heaven received my sweet mother.

There upon my sill you played
Each note with thoughtful skill,
While upon the sea of memories
My tears went and stayed.

You comforted me for such a time
As the world moved swiftly on
When my grief was heavy.
For it alone was mine.

When again I hear your
cunning call
In the whisper of hidden vales,
As an audience of one, I shall
stand and
Wait for your song my heart to
enthrall.

The soft beams of light danced upon the waters. In silent reverence, the hills looked on with pleasant eyes.
The quaint town rested peacefully as the moon and lake took their dance.

Midnight's Mystery

Over the silken laid lake
And sleepy hills of summer's eve
Comes the countenance of a blushing face,
Comes the hymn of a gentle breeze…
The crimson sky
Reveals its starry eyes.

In the midnight hour,
In the watch's silent repose,
I heard the call in the bowers,
I heard no ordinary prose,
Calling from the deep
Twas midnight's mystery.

I saw them come my way
With a graceful stroll
Upon the sweet ballad's sway,
Upon the glassy floor
The beams unfold,
Wavelets of silver and gold.

It was the splendor of the night,
It was the majestic presence of the air
That would woo my fancies into flight
That would keep my spirit there,
Quietly they embrace…
The moon and lake.

The distance rings of the morn,
The water whispers its laments
When silence is broken by the song,
When the moon scatters its waning tints
Sweet dreams…
Until you come again.

Quickly dispersing, the billows exchanged their black, ominous garments for soft white puffs trimmed in golden fringe. Cascades of sun seeped through the breaking clouds upon the vale creating a picturesque scene at the heel of the day.

Take time to do some cloud gazing! You never know what you might see gliding across the sky.

Gliders in the Sky

By hidden threads they glide,
Moving to and fro with no care.
By the mountain's shaded side
Gracefully they wander through the air.
Clouds pure and true
Ride across the sky of blue.

Each one with a pretty face
Adorned in evening's reflection.
Each one to find their place
Amid the stars of Heaven's perfection.
Clouds wispy, soft and light
Riding through summer's night.

They listen for the roar of thunder
To release rain from their folds.
They come together then go asunder
As the moon brushes their hems in gold.
Clouds coming my way
Rest above my head to stay.

With divine expression they take shape
To the patient and watchful eye,
With no notice they vanish to escape
The far horizon without a sigh.
Clouds fancy and free,
Where they go… I want to be.

There are valleys through which every foot must trod that seems to have no end. Every bend in the path is covered by the shadows of sadness as though they seek revenge. The heart in despair cries, "O sun, where doth thou hide"? The soul is heavy with the weight of the storms of life, and searches to find the strength to continue the journey.

I remember being awakened in the watches of the night. The darkness attempted to swallow me and drown all hope. I would cry, pray, and wait for dawn to arrive. One night as I lay awake when sleep and peace eluded me, suddenly, a hope sprang from within the chambers of my spirit. For I realized that it was one feathered friend that would brave the lingering, dark elements to watch for the earliest glimmers of light peeping through the eastern gate. Leaving the comfort of a warm nest, my friend would fly and perch on a lofty platform near my window. My heart would leap with hope as I heard the ballad reminding me the night was done and a new day was birthed. For it is not the entire choir that opens the day, but rather one song that is fresh from Heaven's quill that comes to serenade the listening ear.

No matter how dark the night may be, dawn will always appear when Heaven releases morning's first song.

Morning's First Song

Earth sheds its shadows long
As darkness thins and disappears
When evening's presence will be gone
And the air is sweet and sincere.

In patience I shall wait
With my eye upon the sky
To see the cradle rock and sway
Just before the morning sighs.

For then I know the time is near
When the lonely night must yield
It's passing dreams and hidden fears
To see what the coming day shall wield.

Oh come to me in early glow
While petals are laced in dew
And the day's thoughts are silent and slow
When the heart and soul are renewed.

Swift, I pray your journey will be
As you fan your wings against the dawn
And bring that special word for me
That comes only in morning's first song.

The Magnolia with its versatility is a keeper for every season. Its blossoms, dressed in silky white dresses, are permeated with one of nature's sweetest perfumes. Fall will bring every bird in the forest to feast on the seeded colorful pods while the glossy, green boughs can be worn by any mantle for a Christmas festivity.

Blossoms of White Silk

Her petals were of snowy white
And opened in June's early days
Sending pleasantries along the way
While the day was still quiet.

Even the careless eye
Admired her beauty rare
And stopped to stare
Before the evening drew nigh.

She carried a certain charm
With silken caress leaving
The air with the sweetest breath
To settle in the vale across the farm.

She greeted me thru my pane
Faithfully on each summer's morn
With her dress not the slightest torn
Even after the evening's rain.

Of nature's finest trees
You stand the fairest of all
And fear not the barren fall
When the others lose their leaves.

But every green bough you will keep
Through winter's coming storm
For you it is the norm
Until again spring and summer meet.

Close your eyes and catch the "cloudy train". It will ride upon the wings of the afternoon breeze while the birds and bees are busy with their daily rituals. Allow it to take you to that moment of bliss when you forget the worries of life, and drift deeply in an afternoon's nap! Oh, how sweet it is.

Summer's Drowsy Day

Amid the borders of the passing year
Summer welcomes her drowsy day,
When past is winter's gloom and drear
And the pallet for the weary is laid.

They come from far and wide
To breathe the air's sweetest perfume,
And watch the season display with pride
Her richest and most vibrant blooms.

To then gaze into the vaulted heights,
And catch the ride upon the cloudy train
That shall guide them on the skyward flight
To take them basking in solitude's refrain.

Where each guest comes to gather
And is greeted with a gently kiss,
Before shedding the world's weighty tethers
To rest in the moment's bliss.

For summer's drowsy day I long
When the pallet for me is laid,
And I nap to the rhythm of the soothing song
That summer's afternoon will play.

Fun Facts about the Hummingbird

A "must have" for every serious bird lover is a humming bird feeder. This unique bird is a fascination for many bird watchers. A humming bird can flap its wings about 80 times per second, making a telltale humming noise. They can fly right, left, up, down, backwards, and even upside down. They are also able to hover by flapping their wings in a figure-8 pattern. The humming bird does not use its feet for hopping or walking, but for perching. It's long and tapered bill allows for ease in obtaining nectar from many different sources. "Flower kisser" is the Portuguese name for the humming bird. Their high body temperature and fast heartrate require a large consumption of daily food. They use their tongue to lick their food at a rate of up to 13 licks per second.

One of the most unique things about a humming bird is its iridescent feathers. The design of the structure of the feathers is sophisticated and layered, appearing to change color depending on the angle of the light. Photographers have shot photos of the same humming bird within seconds of each other, but will appear to have different colors especially in the throat area. Some humming birds may have as many as 900 feathers. Truly, they are another one of nature's many wonders.

Hummingbirds/Basic Facts
About Hummingbirds/Defenders of Wildlife
Asknature.org / Mikephoto.com

The Ruby-Collared Dress

Who comes upon my petals to rest,
After the arduous and speedy quest,
Over the ocean and across the shore,
Arrayed in that ruby-collared dress?

Your fanning wings cannot deceive,
Your uncanny hues clear to perceive,
When you come for your sweet delight
After the dreadful winter's eve.

Of your kind, no smaller one nature knows
And every garden their beauty will show
When you come hovering and fluttering,
Your passion upon each blossom to bestow.

Every sanctuary bids you come
To find within their dome nectar's crumbs
While in the garden you dance
And release your pleasant hum.

From petal to petal you travel
To aid other blooms in time of need,
For your purpose is quite unique,
How grateful I am for your faithful deeds.

Hard pressed any traveler would be to not find at least one stately, mighty oak in any southern town. And, so it was in the town in which my husband and I had settled to raise our children. Every time we would pass along the Knox Valley Road, there it stood proud and tall, the Burr Oak that was said to be over 200 years old.

T. Preston Bain wrote the following in The Bugle, a publication of the Brentwood Historic Society. You would be hard pressed to find a citizen in Brentwood who was not familiar with the majestic Burr Oak that stood watch over the open field in front of the library. It stood strong and proud as the world around it evolved and developed. No doubt she enjoyed the many people who found solace and serenity by relaxing or reading underneath her outstretched canopy or the generations of families who joined her for an afternoon picnic. As each day drew to a close she cast her shadow all the way to the banks of The Little Harpeth as if saying goodnight to an old friend and even though she no longer casts a shadow, the memory she casted upon all who saw her will long remain.

Unfortunately, in July of 2010 the beautiful Oak had become very unstable after losing most of its major limbs through a couple of storms. After several attempts by the city to preserve the tree, the battle was lost and the tree removed. But the memory of the Burr Oak lives on today. President of the Tennessee Association of Woodturners, Ray Sandusky, was able to transform the trunk into some unique pieces of art work. Ornamental vases and bowls of all shapes and sizes are some of the artifacts created from the majestic Oak. Mr. Sandusky displayed many of his fine works to the Brentwood Rotary Club in 2011. Later in the year, on April 9 at the Arbor Day celebration, Mr. Sandusky presented to Mayor Betsy Crossley a unique gavel created from the tree.

Even though the majestic tree no longer graces the field by the river with her presence, the remnants of its beauty sits quietly in the homes and offices of those who most adored her.

The Mighty Oak

Thy footing was firmly established
Beneath the lush, green deep
Two centuries before, when from one
Lonely seed thy beauty was conceived.

Strong and steadfast thou hast grown
From the spring rains and
    showering sun,
A beloved statue to all in the
Little village thou hast become.

Whether through the raging storm,
Or beneath the pleasant sky,
Cloaked in dignity, thou stately form
Draws even the careless eye.

From across the way they come,
Their pleaded quilts to spread
To enjoy some shaded fun,
    beneath your
Boughs until the sky is draped in red.

And come around again they will
When the year nears its end,
And to the grassy floor thy scarlet
Memories from the season you
    will send.

My friend, forever its seems thou
    has been,
And oh how well you have aged
As time has dealt gently
In turning each year's page.

Through the village, I shall
    always pass
When on my way to feel that
    gentle stroke
When the wind passes through the
Gracious and noble, mighty oak.

It was nearing dusk on a June evening. The sky cleared and the clouds ran scared. The earth breathed a grateful sigh as each droplet trickled down into the chambers deep. Each petal wore a lustrous coat just before closing for the day. Two of nature's finest events had collided creating a mysterious milky mist across my path.

Indeed, it was an unusual, but creative display of an evening mist. The thickness made it hard to find the way on my regular evening stroll. It was as if it was rising from the earth with a strong and swift decree. It was beautiful and mysterious all in one. I only hoped that I could find my way back to the cottage.

The Milky Mist

Rising from places of the deep,
The milky mist of twilight
Thru wooded vale creeps,
And entangles my feet as it
Beclouds the eyes of night.

It came after the evening rain
When no one was in sight,
As I walked the country lane
And glanced into amber panes,
To brush the eve in pale white.

In silent syllables it speaks
A command for all to yield,
In a voice mysterious and meek,
For those that light would seek,
And to every creature of the field.

It swept the village in surprise,
Bringing a shower of pearls
From the cloud disguised
For the parade of butterflies,
When the morning blooms unfurl.

It mingled through the night,
Between woods and the lake
Causing me to lose sight
Of the coming morning's light
When it would settle in the vale.

Riding on the morning's waves
The wispy clouds heard the sigh,
When the sun opened the day
To disperse the dusky shades
For their time had drawn nigh.

The evening spread a canopy over the sleepy village. Each piece carefully gathered to be knitted together to release a proclamation of peace over every troubled soul.

A Night's Canopy

I look upon your evening's face
And feel your peaceful stance
And the wonder of your glance
To marvel at your starry maze.

For a moment I will try
To number just a few
As though it were something new
To then ask myself why?

For some reign bright
While others tend to wander
And eventually go asunder
Never shining through the night.

What was it, I thought?
That caused the memories to banish
And my restless pulse to vanish
What the day had brought?

Could it be the willow's breeze,
Or the sweet perfume
Of the evening's blooms?
Could someone tell me please?

Of these things I can be sure
To my soul you bring a sweet release
As you send your calming ease,
And that your beauty forever endures.

So beneath your canopy I will lay
And wait your counsel to hear
To come and wipe away the tears
So I may greet the coming day.

After the Rain

Doth not the air share her pleasant scents
After the lowly clouds their heads have bent
To pour through the crystal pitcher
Streams of showers from Heaven's cistern?

And the sounds are spoken soft
As majestic colors in the bow are caught,
When the lays come pure and clear
To all earth's listening ear.

Clouds part their wondering ways,
The golden eye dims her rays
Steeping the hills in a purple mist,
Nature rests in the moment of bliss.

Hills and forests breathe a grateful sigh,
For blooms in the vale can now close their eyes
And rest beneath evening's starry train
That comes sweet and soft after the rain.

Summer's Sonnet

In slippers soft and silent
Came the final steps of day.
Velvet, rose, purple, and gold
They swayed across the lake

The sleepy sky yawned
Weary from the summer's heat
As the sun bowed and
Remnants danced with graceful feet.

A canopy of light lingered
To cover them fair
As they strolled my way
Down the evening stairs.

A summer's sonnet I thought,
In brilliant and vivid tones
With a peaceful message,
They came not alone.

To rest, my eyes gave way
As the dream called me in,
There by the glassy lake
Beside my faithful friend.

Accompanied by strains
Of the misty breeze
A summer's sonnet was penned, of
Moments sublime, my favorite are these!